101 KNOCK KNOCK JOKES

VOLUME 2

THE HENNESSY KIDS

Featured Artwork by KATHERINE HENNESSY

Featured Artwork by SAMUEL HENNESSY

Featured Artwork by DANIEL HENNESSY

The Hennessy Entertainment
Company

101 Knock Knock Jokes Vol. 2 / by The Hennessy Kids

ISBN 978-1-989621-06-6 (Print)

ISBN 978-1-989621-07-3 (E-book)

1. Wit and humor, Juvenile. 2. English wit and humor. I. The Hennessy Kids, author

The Hennessy Entertainment Company | HennessyEnt.com

To Grammie and Grampie, we love you!

1

NAME JOKES

Knock, knock.
    Who's there?
    Dwayne.
    Dwayne who.
    Dwayne the Knock Johnson.

Knock, knock.
    Who's there?
    Tish.
    Tish who?
    Yes, thank you, I need to blow my nose.

Knock, knock.
    Who's there?
    Sadie.
    Sadie who?
    Sadie magic words and I'll tell you.

Knock, knock.
    Who's there?
    Horton hears a.
    Horton hears a who?
    Hey, I like that Dr. Seuss book, too.

Knock, knock.
    Who's there?
    Rufus.
    Rufus who?
    Rufus leaking and I'm getting wet.

Knock, knock.
    Who's there?
    Ada.
    Ada who?
    Ada lot for breakfast and now I'm going to throw up.

Knock, knock.
    Who's there?
    Hugo.
    Hugo who?
    Hugo your way, and I'll go mine.

Knock, knock.
    Who's there?
    Colleen.
    Colleen who?
    Colleen up your room, it's a mess.

Knock, knock.
> Who's there?
> Chuck.
> Chuck who?
> I'm here to chuck wood, don't ask me how much.

Knock, knock.
> Who's there?
> Allison.
> Allison who?
> Allison to my music all day long.

Knock, knock.
> Who's there?
> Pete.
> Pete who?
> Pete-za delivery.

Knock, knock.
> Who's there?
> Norma Lee.
> Norma Lee who?
> Norma Lee I have my keys with me to open this door.

Knock, knock.
> Who's there?
> Hugh.
> Hugh who?
> Hugh can't fool me, I'm not telling.

Knock, knock.
  Who's there?
  Fiona.
  Fiona who?
  Fiona of the house is in, I'd like to speak with him.

Knock, knock.
  Who's there?
  Duncan.
  Duncan who?
  Duncan your chickens before they hatch.

Knock, knock.
  Who's there?
  Mary Lee.
  Mary Lee who?
  Mary Lee, Mary Lee, life is but a dream. Row, Row, row your
boat.

Knock, knock.
  Who's there?
  Ringo.
  Ringo who?
  Ringo round the roses.

Knock, knock.
  Who's there?
  Al.
  Al who?
  Al give you a surprise if you open this door.

Knock, knock.
> Who's there?
> Champ.
> Champ who?
> Shampoo your hair to make it soft and shiny.

Knock, knock.
> Who's there?
> Theodore.
> Theodore who?
> Theodore is stuck, please help me open it.

Knock, knock.
> Who's there?
> Les.
> Les who?
> Les go out for a picnic.

Knock, knock.
> Who's there?
> Sid.
> Sid who?
> Sid down. It's time to eat.

Knock, knock.
> Who's there?
> Philip.
> Philip who?
> Philip my gas tank, please, I've got a long way to go.

Knock, knock.
Who's there?
Rena.
Rena who?
Rena this bell doesn't seem to do any good.

Knock, knock.
Who's there?
Rita.
Rita who?
Rita book from the library every week and you'll get smart.

Knock, knock.
Who's there?
Henrietta.
Henrietta who?
Henrietta worm that was in his apple.

Knock, knock.
Who's there?
Wayne.
Wayne who?
Wayne, Wayne, go away, come again another day.

Knock, knock.
Who's there?
Isadore.
Isadore who?
Is the doorbell ringing?

FEATURED ARTWORK #1

Who loves you? Owl does. Artwork by Katherine Hennessy

2

FOOD JOKES

Knock, knock.
 Who's there?
 Broccoli
 Broccoli who?
 Broccoli doesn't have a last name, silly.

Knock, knock.
 Who's there?
 Cereal.
 Cereal who?
 Cereal pleasure to meet you.

Knock, knock.
 Who's there?
 Butter.
 Butter who?
 Butter let me in, it's raining out here.

Knock, knock.
>   Who's there?
>   Peas.
>   Peas who?
>   Peas to meet you.

Knock, knock.
>   Who's there?
>   Ice cream soda.
>   Ice cream soda who?
>   Ice scream soda whole world can hear me.

Knock, knock.
>   Who's there?
>   Water.
>   Water who?
>   Water you waiting for, please open the door.

Knock, knock.
>   Who's there?
>   Della.
>   Della who?
>   Dellacatessen is a tasty place to get some food.

Knock, knock.
>   Who's there?
>   Doughnut
>   Doughnut who?
>   Doughnut disturb me, I like my quiet time.

Knock, knock.
>Who's there?
>Sweden.
>Sweden who?
>Sweden the lemonade, it's too sour.

Knock, knock.
>Who's there?
>Jelly.
>Jelly who?
>Jellycopter, jellycopter.

Knock, knock.
>Who's there?
>Lettuce.
>Lettuce who?
>Lettuce in and you'll find out.

Knock, knock.
>Who's there?
>Loaf.
>Loaf who?
>I don't just like bread, I loaf it.

Knock, knock.
>Who's there?
>Eat.
>Eat who?
>Eat your veggies.

Knock, knock.
    Who's there?
    Muffin.
    Muffin who?
    Muffin the matter with me, how about you?

Knock, knock.
    Who's there?
    Ice cream.
    Ice cream who?
    Ice cream if you don't let me in.

Knock, knock.
    Who's there?
    Pudding.
    Pudding who?
    Pudding your shoes on before your pants is not a good idea.

Knock, knock.
    Who's there?
    Candy.
    Candy who?
    Candy cow jump over the moon?

Knock, knock.
    Who's there?
    Donut.
    Donut who?
    I donut know, you tell me.

Knock, knock.
Who's there?
Orange.
Orange who?
Orange you glad there is no school on Saturday?

Knock, knock.
Who's there?
Turnip.
Turnip who?
Turnip your doorbell volume, I've been ringing it forever.

Knock, knock.
Who's there?
Honeydew.
Honeydew who?
Honeydew your homework before you go outside.

Knock, knock.
Who's there?
Butter.
Butter who?
Butter bring an umbrella, it looks like rain.

Knock, knock.
Who's there?
Pudding.
Pudding who?
Pudding in your face.

Knock, knock.
    Who's there?
    Nacho.
    Nacho who?
    Nacho cheese, so give it back.

FEATURED ARTWORK #2

Octopus will make you laugh with ten tickles. Artwork by Katherine Hennessy

3

NATURE JOKES

Knock, knock.
>Who's there?
>Leaf.
>Leaf who?
>Leaf me alone.

Knock, knock.
>Who's there?
>Cows go.
>Cows go who?
>Cows go moo, not who.

Knock, knock.
>Who's there?
>Hoo.
>Hoo who?
>You sure talk like an owl.

Knock, knock.
    Who's there?
    Goat.
    Goat who?
    Goat on a limb and open the door.

Knock, knock.
    Who's there?
    Lion.
    Lion who?
    Lion out in the sun on your doorstep, it's nice outside.

Knock, knock.
    Who's there?
    Dragon.
    Dragon who?
    Dragon your feet again, hurry up and open the door.

Knock, knock.
    Who's there?
    Ducks.
    Ducks who?
    Ducks don't go who, they go quack.

Knock, knock.
    Who's there?
    Yorkies.
    Yorkies who?
    Yorkies don't fit in the lock.

Knock, knock.
>Who's there?
>Toucan.
>Toucan who?
>Toucan play that game.

Knock, knock.
>Who's there?
>Wood ant.
>Wood ant who?
>Wood ant you like to know.

Knock, knock.
>Who's there?
>Owls.
>Owls who?
>Exactly.

Knock, knock.
>Who's there?
>Hello.
>Hello who?
>Hello kitty.

Knock, knock.
>Who's there?
>Baby Owl.
>Baby Owl who?
>Baby, owl see you later.

Knock, knock.
    Who's there?
    Iguana.
    Iguane who?
    Iguana come in.

Knock, knock.
    Who's there?
    Safari.
    Safari who?
    Safari so good.

Knock, knock.
    Who's there?
    Flea.
    Flea who?
    Fleas a jolly good fellow.

Knock, knock.
    Who's there?
    Owl.
    Owl who?
    Owl aboard, the train is leaving.

Knock, knock.
    Who's there?
    Nana.
    Nana who?
    Nana your bee's wax.

Knock, knock.
>Who's there?
>Gopher.
>Gopher who?
>I could go for a cup of hot chocolate right about now.

Knock, knock.
>Who's there?
>Laughing tentacles.
>Laughing tentacles who?
>You would laugh too, if I gave you tentacles.

Knock, knock.
>Who's there?
>Quacker.
>Quacker who?
>Quacker another bad joke and I'm leaving.

Knock, knock.
>Who's there?
>Kanga.
>Kanga who?
>Close, it's kangaroo.

Knock, knock.
>Who's there?
>Herring.
>Herring who?
>Herring a lot of funny knock knock jokes today.

Knock, knock.
     Who's there?
     A cow with no lips.
     A cow with no lips who?
     A cow with no lips says ooo ooo.

Knock, knock.
     Who's there?
     Honey bee.
     Honey bee who?
     Honey, bee a good friend and let me in.

Knock, knock.
     Who's there?
     Thumpin'.
     Thumpin' who?
     Thumpin' green and slimy is crawling on your shoulder.

FEATURED ARTWORK #3

This animal is the Greatest Of All Time. Artwork by Samuel Hennessy

4

MORE NAME JOKES

Knock, knock.
   Who's there?
   Henrietta.
   Henrietta who?
   Henrietta worm that was in his apple.

Knock, knock.
   Who's there?
   Wayne.
   Wayne who?
   Wayne, Wayne, go away, come again some other day.

Knock, knock.
   Who's there?
   Hello.
   Hello who?
   My name is not Who.

Knock, knock.
 Who's there?
 Sarah.
 Sarah who?
 Sarah way you could let me in?

Knock, knock.
 Who's there?
 Noah.
 Noah who?
 Noah good place to get a key for this door?

Knock, knock.
 Who's there?
 Heidi.
 Heidi who?
 Heidi-clare thumb war on you.

Knock, knock.
 Who's there?
 Harvey.
 Harvey who?
 How long Harvey going to play this game?

Knock, knock.
 Who's there?
 Irene.
 Irene who?
 Irene and Irene but still no one answers the door.

Knock, knock.
>Who's there?
>Queen.
>Queen who?
>Queen as a whistle.

Knock, knock.
>Who's there?
>Alex.
>Alex who?
>Just let me in, Alex-splain later.

Knock, knock.
>Who's there?
>Annie.
>Annie who?
>Annie time you want to open this door would be good.

Knock, knock.
>Who's there?
>Saul.
>Saul who?
>Saul the King's horses and all the King's men.

Knock, knock.
>Who's there?
>Stan.
>Stan who?
>Stan back, I'm about to open the door.

Knock, knock.
    Who's there?
    Toby.
    Toby who?
    Toby or not Toby, that is the question.

Knock, knock.
    Who's there?
    Sam.
    Sam who?
    Sam person who answered the door last time.

Knock, knock.
    Who's there?
    Karim.
    Karim who?
    Karim of the crop.

Knock, knock.
    Who's there?
    Wanda.
    Wanda who?
    Wanda where I put my car keys.

Knock, knock.
    Who's there?
    Wendy.
    Wendy who?
    Wendy door opens you'll find out.

Knock, knock.
>Who's there?
>Xavier.
>Xavier who?
>Xavier breath, I don't want to talk right now.

Knock, knock.
>Who's there?
>Leena.
>Leena who?
>Leena little closer and I will tell you.

Knock, knock.
>Who's there?
>Tinkerbell.
>Tinkerbell who?
>Think your bell is out of order, that's why I'm knocking.

Knock, knock.
>Who's there?
>Scott.
>Scott who?
>Scott nothing to do with you.

Knock, knock.
>Who's there?
>Adam.
>Adam who?
>Adam up and send me the bill.

Knock, Knock.
    Who's there?
    Abbey.
    Abbey who?
    A bee stung me on my bum.

Knock, knock.
    Who's there?
    Howie.
    Howie who?
    I'm fine, how are you?

FEATURED ARTWORK #4

Bee kind. Artwork by Daniel Hennessy

WORD SEARCH

```
D H Y F W C N G T A Y Y I A T
F V A E K O G S O D D J L A B
I E Q N A K C U D N I E O Y O
L E O B U T T E R A X G C P H
P C N S N U J O H W J A C U C
K I G Y E G N A R O N S O D A
A M N I A T P F H D U I R D N
L I W R B W I R Y F C A B I E
L O X A U O D W U A S H I N W
I Z M F N T X R A D A A U G T
S P M A H C S C O T T J R C Q
O R E S E H E N R I E T T A K
N Q W M I N A C U O T R N D H
E F Z Y D Y O R K I E S R P N
N P D R I Y D N E W A P S C X
```

ADA	FIONA	SAFARI
ALEX	GOAT	SARAH
ALLISON	HEIDI	SCOTT
BROCCOLI	HENRIETTA	TOUCAN
BUTTER	KNOCK	TURNIP
CANDY	LEAF	WANDA
CHAMP	NACHO	WATER
CHUCK	ORANGE	WENDY
DUCK	PUDDING	WHO
DWAYNE	RUFUS	YORKIES

6

YOUR FAVOURITE JOKE

What is your favourite knock knock joke that isn't in this book?

Send it to us at thehennessykids@gmail.com, and we'll look to share it online with all our friends.

ACKNOWLEDGMENTS

Special thank you to everybody who is getting our joke books out from their public library and then sharing jokes with their family and friends!

Thank you for reading our book! We hope you enjoyed it.
Please tell these jokes to your friends and family and make more
people happy.

ABOUT THE AUTHORS

The Hennessy Kids think the world would be better with more smiles.

Want to know when our new books and games are available? Sign up for our newsletter or visit www.hennessyent.com!

BOOKS BY THE HENNESSY KIDS

101 Funny Jokes, Vol. 1

101 Funny Jokes, Vol. 2

101 Pet Jokes

101 Knock Knock Jokes, Vol. 1

101 Knock Knock Jokes, Vol. 2

101 Knock Knock Jokes, Vol. 3

The Big Book Of Jokes

101 Nature Jokes

101 Food Jokes

101 Halloween Jokes

101 Christmas Jokes

101 School Jokes

Visit hennessyent.com for the complete up-to-date list of our books and games!